□ NATIONAL GEOGRAPHIC CHANNEL

GREAT MIGRATIONS

Elephants

Laura Marsh

□ NATIONAL
GEOGRAPHIC

Washington, D.C.

For Jackie, Billy, Jane, and Lilly—L.F.M

Published by National Geographic Partners, LLC, Washington, D.C. 20036
All rights reserved. Reproduction in whole or in part without written permission of the publisher is prohibited.

Library of Congress Cataloging-in-Publication Data
Marsh, Laura F.
Great migrations. Elephants / by Laura Marsh.
p. cm.
Includes index.
ISBN 978-1-4263-0743-0 (pbk. : alk. paper) -- ISBN 978-1-4263-0744-7 (library binding : alk. paper)
1. African elephant--Migration--Juvenile literature. I. Title.
QL737.P98M3697 2010
599.67'41568--dc22
2010017961

Abbreviation Key: GET = Getty Images; IS = iStockphoto.com; NGS = NationalGeographicStock.com; NGT = National Geographic Television; SS = Shutterstock.com

Elephants marching throughout, Carlton Ward Jr; Background elephant skin throughout, Fedor Selivanov/ SS; Weighty Word throughout: Jason Prince/ SS; Cover, Carlton Ward Jr; 1, Carlton Ward Jr; 2, Jason Prince/ SS; 4, Carlton Ward Jr; 5 (bottom), NGT; 5 (top), John Eastcott and Yva Momatiuk/ NGS; 6 (center), Paul Souders/ Corbis; 8-9 (center), Kenneth C. Zirkel/ IS; 10, Galyna Andrushko/ SS; 11 (right), Jodi Cobb/ NGS;11 (top), Michael Gray/ IS; 11 (center), enviromantic/ IS; 11 (bottom), itographer/ IS; 12 (center), Carlton Ward Jr; 15, Carlton Ward Jr; 16 (top), Carlton Ward Jr; 16 (bottom), Carlton Ward Jr; 17 (top), Carlton Ward Jr; 17 (bottom), Carlton Ward Jr; 18, Jim Kruger/ IS; 19 (top), Carlton Ward Jr; 19 (bottom), Carlton Ward Jr; 20-21, Winfried Wisniewski/ Corbis; 22-23 (center), Carlton Ward Jr; 24 (bottom center), Michael Nichols/ NGS; 25 (center), Carlton Ward Jr; 26 (bottom center), Michael Nichols/ NGS; 27, Martin Harvey/ Gallo Images/ Corbis; 28, Michael Nichols/ NGS; 29, Michael Nichols/ NGS; 31 (center), Michael Nichols/ NGS; 32 (top left), Michael Nichols/ NGS; 32 (top right), Slobo Mitic/ IS; 32 (center left), IS; 32 (center right), Michael Nichols/ NGS; 32 (bottom left), Jodi Cobb/ NGS; 32 (bottom right), Javarman/ SS; 33 (top left), Michael Nichols/ NGS; 33 (top right), Carlton Ward Jr; 33 (center left), Carlton Ward Jr; 33 (center right), Michael Nichols/ NGS; 33 (bottom), Michael Nichols/ NGS; 34-35, Carlton Ward Jr; 36-37, Carlton Ward Jr; 37, Gerry Ellis/ Minden Pictures/ NGS; 38, Gunnar Pippel/ SS; 39, Carlton Ward Jr; 41, Michael Nichols/ NGS; 42, Yuriy Korchagin/ IS; 43 (bottom center), Tim Fitzharris/ Minden Pictures/ NGS; 43 (top right), Jason Prince/ SS; 44 (bottom center), Norie Quintos/ NGS;46 (center left), Micheal Nichols/ NGS; 46 (top right), Carlton Ward Jr; 46 (bottom left), Galyna Andrushko/ SS; 46 (center right), Jodi Cobb/ NGS; 46 (bottom right), Carlton Ward Jr; 47 (top left), Carlton Ward Jr; 47 (top right), Michael Nichols/ NGS; 47 (center left), Gerry Ellis/ MInden Pictures/ NGS; 47 (bottom left), Richard Cano/ IS; 47 (bottom right), Carlton Ward Jr

National Geographic supports K–12 educators with ELA Common Core Resources.
Visit natgeoed.org/commoncore for more information.

Printed in the United States of America
16/WOR/8

Table of Contents

On the Move

When animals travel from one region or habitat to another, it is called migration. Animals migrate in search of food or a mate. Migration helps animals survive on Earth.

Many animals migrate. The Mali elephant is one of them.

elephants

wildebeest

red crabs

Weighty Words

MIGRATION: Moving from one region or habitat to another for food or a mate

MATE: Either a male or female in a pair. Most animals need a mate to have babies.

What animal . . .

Can travel up to 90 miles a day?

Has tusks used to dig for water and find food?

Is the largest land animal on Earth?

An elephant!

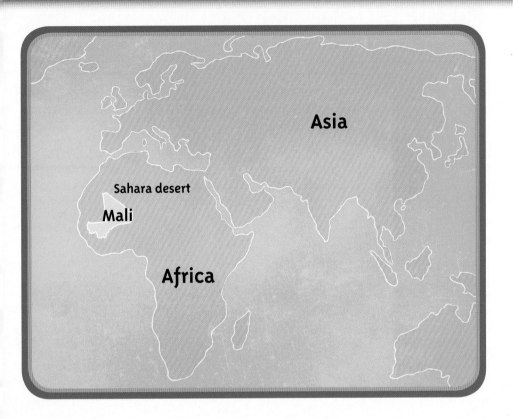

Elephants live in Africa and Asia. This book is about the elephants that live on the southern border of the Sahara desert in Mali, West Africa.

How Do We Measure Up?

An African elephant is so big, it makes a six-foot-tall man look small.

7

Everything African Elephant

SKIN: Wrinkled and gray. Elephants spray water and dust over their skin to stay cool in the hot sun.

HEIGHT:
8–13 feet tall

WEIGHT:
5,000–14,000 pounds

LIFE SPAN:
Up to 70 years

SIZE:
Largest land animal on Earth

FEET: Hooved, with spongy pads that absorb weight

EARS: Keep elephants cool by releasing heat

TUSKS: Used to dig for water and for roots to eat. They are also used to strip bark from trees for a tasty meal.

TRUNK: It's used for smelling, drinking, breathing, trumpeting, and spraying water over the elephant's body. It has two fingerlike ends for grabbing.

Enormous Appetites

Elephants are herbivores. They eat only plants, such as roots, grasses, fruit, and bark. Elephants need to eat a lot to fuel their massive bodies—up to 300 pounds per day. That's like eating 1,200 hamburgers!

The Mali elephants' habitat is the woodland area near watering holes.

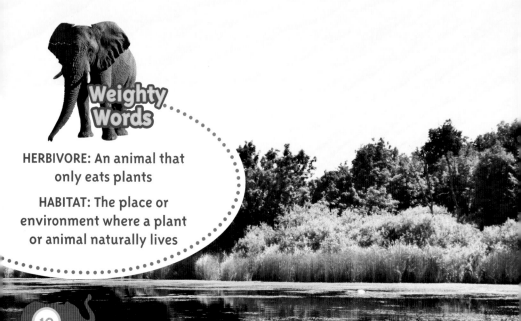

Weighty Words

HERBIVORE: An animal that only eats plants

HABITAT: The place or environment where a plant or animal naturally lives

tree bark

papayas

grass

11

Sticking Together

Female elephants and young elephants form a group called a herd. Herds are led by an older female and usually have 6 to 20 elephants. But in some areas, much larger herds have been seen.

Females stay with the same herd their whole lives. But males only remain with the herd until they are 12 to 15 years old. Then they join a group of other males, called a bachelor herd, or live alone.

Male and female herds migrate separately.

Elephants Never Forget

Scientists think that elephants have good memories. Herd leaders remember where the best watering holes are, even if they have not been there in several years.

Weighty Word

HERD: A large group of wild animals

Tough Travel

Mali elephants migrate farther than any other elephants. Scientists estimate they travel between 280 and 435 miles. Traveling 435 miles is like walking from Washington, D.C. to New York City and back every year!

weird but true
Elephants sleep standing up.

435 miles round trip

Washington, D.C.   New York City

Elephant Mileage

Scientists are able to find out how far an elephant travels by attaching a GPS tracking collar around its neck. The elephant is given medicine to make it fall asleep so that the scientists can safely attach the collar. When the elephant wakes up, it joins the herd and goes on its way.

Full Circle

The Mali elephants start and end their journey at Lake Banzena. It contains the only year-round watering hole in the area. All other watering holes disappear during the dry season.

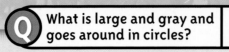

The elephants spend the dry season at Lake Banzena. But by April and May there is little food at Banzena because elephants and other animals have eaten it. It is time to move on.

When the rainy season begins, the elephants travel south. The rain renews old watering holes and allows nutritious new food to grow elsewhere.

Weighty Word

INSTINCT: Behavior that animals are born knowing how to do

Perfect Timing

The elephants begin their migration south as soon as the first rain begins. They know by instinct that it's time to migrate.

19

The elephants eat the plants around a small watering hole and then move on. They travel from watering hole to watering hole for many months. Their route makes a big circle.

By November, the rains stop and it's time to return to Lake Banzena, where they spend another dry season. But the elephants must hurry before the watering holes along the way dry up. They can't live without water.

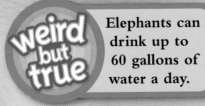

weird but true

Elephants can drink up to 60 gallons of water a day.

21

Baby Elephants

When baby elephants are born, they weigh about 200 pounds. That's as much as a large adult man.

Newborn elephants are three feet tall—about the height of a sofa.

Baby elephants are called calves. They drink their mother's milk until they are four or five years old. Calves might suck on their trunks for comfort, just like babies suck their thumbs.

Weighty Word

CALF:
A baby elephant

25

Elephant Talk

weird but true

Elephants can make more than 25 separate sounds that mean different things.

Elephants use different parts of their bodies to gather and send information.

They use their mouths and trunks to grumble, growl, and trumpet. This is how they talk to each other.

Sniffing Out Danger

Scientists stay downwind from elephants when they study them. Do you know why? Because if they don't, the elephants will smell their scent and run off.

Elephants use their trunks to smell if other animals are nearby. If they sense danger, they call to each other. Then the adults circle around the young elephants to protect them.

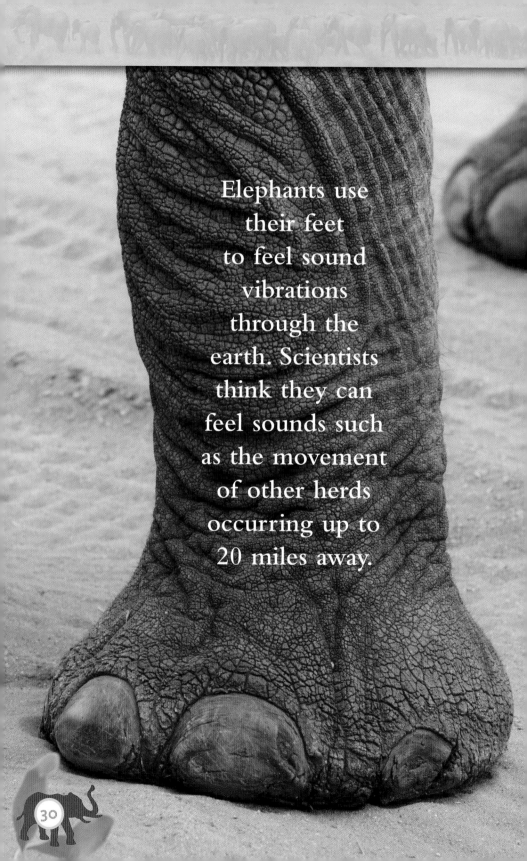

Elephants use their feet to feel sound vibrations through the earth. Scientists think they can feel sounds such as the movement of other herds occurring up to 20 miles away.

Elephants use their trunks to greet each other and show affection. Sometimes they hook their trunks together in a kind of elephant hug.

10 Cool Things About Elephants

1 Elephants can weigh as much as 7½ tons — more than two large SUVs.

2 Elephants don't sleep much. They need to spend a lot of time looking for food.

3 They make loud, low sounds that other elephants can hear up to six miles away.

4 Their ears give off heat to keep them cool in hot temperatures.

5 Mother elephants are pregnant for 22 months. That's almost two years!

6

Unlike human newborns, calves can stand within an hour of birth.

7

They can run as fast as 25 miles an hour and travel up to 120 miles in one day.

8

Each elephant's ears are different. Scientists can tell individual elephants by their ear shapes and markings.

9

Elephants favor their right or left tusk—just like we favor our right or left hand.

10

A herd leader makes all decisions for the herd, such as where to go and when to stop, eat, and drink.

Elephant Emergency

More than 1,000 elephants once roamed all across Mali. Now there are fewer than 400 elephants.

What happened to the Mali elephants?

weird but true

An elephant's tusks keep growing throughout its adult life.

1,000 elephants

400 elephants

Now

Then

= 100 elephants

Poachers killed many elephants in the 1970s and 1980s. They only wanted the elephants' tusks and sold them at high prices.

Although poaching is outlawed, it is still a problem today.

 weird but true

An elephant's trunk has about 100,000 different muscles, but no bones.

Elephant tusks are made of ivory, which has been used to make things like jewelry and piano keys.

Mali elephants are trying to survive in difficult conditions. There is less water and fewer plants than there used to be. One reason is because the Earth has become warmer. Higher temperatures are drying up water sources.

But people are making it harder for elephants, too. They are settling where elephants live and migrate. So there is less and less land for the elephants. Also, livestock owned by local people are eating plants and drinking water that elephants need, too.

Q Why was the elephant asked to leave the swimming pool?

A He couldn't hold up his trunks.

Weighty Word

LIVESTOCK: Animals raised to sell or use

39

Helping Mali Elephants

Scientists are keeping track of the number of elephants so that if elephant numbers go down, they can find a solution before it's too late.

Scientists are also tagging elephants with special collars to track them. The collars show scientists exactly where the elephants travel. Then people can build roads and homes elsewhere. This will create safe migration paths for the elephants.

weird but true

An elephant's skin can be one inch thick in some areas.

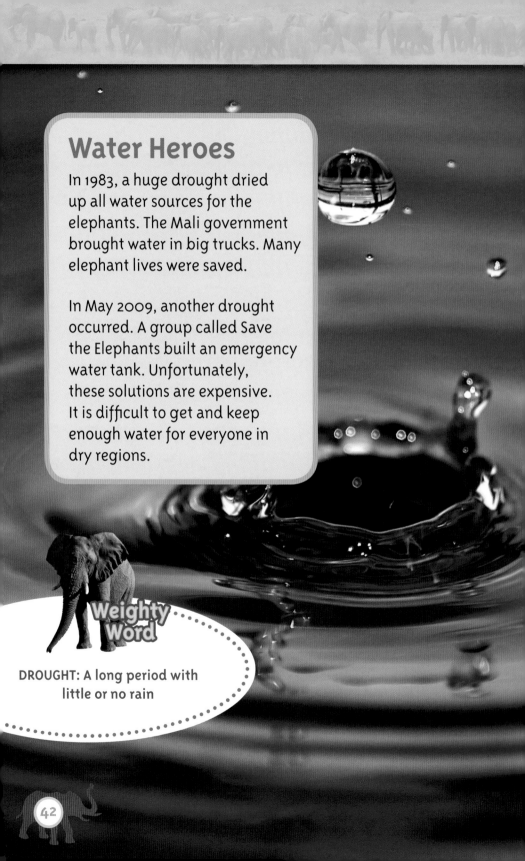

Water Heroes

In 1983, a huge drought dried up all water sources for the elephants. The Mali government brought water in big trucks. Many elephant lives were saved.

In May 2009, another drought occurred. A group called Save the Elephants built an emergency water tank. Unfortunately, these solutions are expensive. It is difficult to get and keep enough water for everyone in dry regions.

Weighty
Word

DROUGHT: A long period with little or no rain

There is protected reserve land
where elephants can live.
But only a small part
of the elephants' range
is on this land. More
protected land is needed.

Local people in the Mali government want the elephants to survive. Mali children learn about the elephants in school. The more people know, the better we can help the elephants.

What You Can Do

To learn more about Mali elephants and their amazing migration, check out these organizations that help them.

Living With Elephants

http://www.livingwithelephants.org

National Geographic Society

http://kids.nationalgeographic.com/Animals/
CreatureFeature/African-elephant

Save the Elephants

http://www.savetheelephants.org

The WILD Foundation

http://www.wild.org/field-projects/
the-desert-elephants-of-mali

Glossary

MATE: Either a male or female in a pair. Most animals need a mate to have babies.

MIGRATION: Moving from one region or habitat to another for food or a mate

INSTINCT: Behavior that animals are born knowing how to do

CALF: A baby elephant

POACHER: Someone who hunts animals illegally

HABITAT: The place or environment where a plant or animal naturally lives

HERBIVORE: An animal that only eats plants

HERD: A large group of wild animals

LIVESTOCK: Animals raised to sell or use

DROUGHT: A long period with little or no rain

Index